Words Strung along the Left Margin

James A. F. Stoner

Words Strung along the Left Margin

ISBN (9798844211966)

Printed in USA by

Dedication

To my life's muses
Barbara, Alexandra,
Carolyn, et al

Table of Contents

Introduction

For me, the title of this book says it all. These words strung along the left margin are simply words that speak to me. Perhaps some of them will speak to others.

The words come from a variety of places. Many of them are in my still-unfinished novella *Five to Five*. Some are from my life and fantasies; some from the lives and dreams of others. Some are inspired by a friend's poems and many by events happening around all of us.

I have been blessed with many opportunities to teach in executive programs, largely because of the introductions, support, and coaching provided by good friends Tom Ference and George Farris. One time, maybe more than one time, a very senior executive said that if he got one good idea that he used from a program, the week was well spent. I hope you find at least one set of words in this slim volume that speak to you, and perhaps that you use in some way.

HAIKU

Spring Lives in Your Smile

Spring lives in your smile

You are the summer and fall

Without you: winter

Winter Moon Sleeps Late

Winter moon sleeps late

Cold seas rise and fall evermore

Morning arrives soon

She is Our Cupid

She is Our Cupid
Reminding me ev'ry day
Of my joy with you

Closet Muse

My muse refuses
to be named, but without her
no poems, no novel

A Virus (Pandemic) Haiku

For many of us
Binary confinement's worse
Than solitary

Taxes

Need to file taxes
Inspires diligent action
on everything else.

Taxes overdue.
Must do everything else.
Procrastination.

The six haiku included in the unpresidented series were written in the early days following the election that saved the country from Mr. Trump's continuing to defile the office of the President of the United States. When they were written many others and I were experiencing what we thought was the end of the pain he visited upon so many millions and the death sentences his and his supporters' incompetence, mendacity, and villainy perpetrated on so many Americans.

Hopefully, some day he and his hero Vladimir Putin will finally be gone – words written in late February2022 as Putin follows in the footsteps of Adolph Hitler.

UnPresidented Haiku – written at an optimistic time

1

Coronavirus kills

Most vulnerable of us

And Donald Trump plays golf

2

Un Pres i dent ed
Our White House cleansed of worst evil
America heals

3

Amen, Trump is gone
Worst of evils gone at last
Healing begins now

4

Mar-a-lago's loss
Is America's great gain
Good riddance for sure

5

When he's gone, I said

Birds sing, sun shines, flowers bloom,

Jeez sus, I was right

6

Ten days, one hundred

We healed more than, faster than

Anyone ever hoped.

Mini clarification

In the "Tailgaters" haiku, the word tailgaters refers to folks who are driving too closely to the rear end of your car. It does not refer to folks who are picnicking off the tailgate of their station wagon or SUV at a Saturday football game. Those folks are fine.

Life’s Major Choices

Life’s major choices
Long life or potato chips
No-brainer for me

Five, Seven, and Five Haiku

Five seven and five
Counting syllables all day
Many thanks to google

If it Can’t Be Said

If it can't be said
in seventeen syllables
Is it worth saying?

MacBook Air is Kind

MacBookAir is kind
And when it is not it is
A four-letter word

Tailgaters

Let tailgaters pass
With one asshole behind us
Who needs another?

Hornet’s Nests Haiku

Our hornets’ nests from
Unresolved violations
Waiting to be poked

My current partner
Pokes hornets’ nests we both forged
Leaves me to be stung

ENTP Haiku Commentary

These three haiku were inspired by the Myer's-Briggs Type Indicator, a widely used vehicle for gaining perspective on ourselves and others.

The MBTI is based on our responses to a series of questions in which we report how we see ourselves. On March 6, 2022, in "definitions of MBTI types" Google stated:

"*(The MBTI) ... indicates your personality preferences in four dimensions: Where you focus your attention – Extraversion (E) or Introversion (I) The way you take in information – Sensing (S) or INtuition (N) How you make decisions – Thinking (T) or Feeling (F) How you deal with the world – Judging (J) or Perceiving (P)*"

Although not everyone has a high respect for the MBTI, I do and have had much fun and considerable playful insight into myself and others from being with it and sharing it with others for many decades.

These three haiku are inspired by my MBTI scores and my interpretations of them. My scores are ENTP – extroverted, intuitive, thinking, perceiving type. According to

https://eu.themyersbriggs.com/en/tools/MBTI/MBTI-personality-Types/ENTP Accessed 3/6/22

"ENTPs solve problems creatively and are often innovative in their way of thinking, seeing connections and patterns within a system. They enjoy developing strategy and often spot and capitalize on new opportunities that present themselves."

"ENTPs sometimes avoid making decisions and may become excited about ideas that are not feasible because of constraints on time or resources. They may be overly challenging to others and their ideas."

"ENTPs are typically emergent, theoretical and flexible as well as imaginative and challenging."

ENTP Haiku

We ENTPs
Don't know what we think 'til we
hear ourselves say it.

We don't understand
What we mean until we see
What we have written.

And we do not know
What we communicated
Until you tell us.

Pandemic Haiku

Since the pandemic
One blink, and a week is gone
Two blinks: a month's gone

Lepidoptera Haiku

Lep·i·dop·ter·a
Become moths or butterflies
Such a difference

LOVE POEMS

Lying Mirrors

When I feel good
about myself
I know that I look like
a cross of Robert Redford
and Paul Newman.

Knowing that
makes me feel really good
because looks are
so important to me.

Much too important
Much too important
Much too important
to me.

But all mirrors are liars
at least to me.

Sometimes, mistakenly,
I am foolish enough
to look into the mirror.

Some stranger stares back at me.
A stranger who does not look like
Robert Redford
or Paul Newman
or both.

I try to avoid mirrors
and frankly
I'm pretty successful

They all seem to lie.
All of them.

I do wish
I could find
a mirror that tells the truth.
Shows that I am really
that Redford/Newman combination.

When I'm with you,
and things are good with us.
As they usually are,
Sometimes
I see that that true mirror
in your eyes.

George Bernard Shaw

Supposedly
George Bernard Shaw,
author, playwright, liberal/socialist,
polemicist, political activist, feminist,
champion of the poor and vulnerable,
success,
was asked
late in life,
If he could be anyone in the world ever,
who would he choose to be?

I think often
of his answer:

The man I could have been.

With you,
only with you,
I feel as though I am
The man I could have been.

Competing

You know I'm not competing,
but I am
with ghosts.

You say I've already won
the competition
that never happened.

The Mensa genius
exploding your life
in the file room,
hearing the unseen
hours of rapture,
the surprise ring,
and the departure
before the realities
and routines of daily life
and their toll.

The wounded aviator,
The word "fantastic"
explaining
abuse
and writing on my mind
the unreachable standard.

You know I'm not competing,
but I am.

I cannot win against a ghost
I am not a Mensa genius with a video camera
nor a 6 foot-four aviator shrinking to a dwarf
as you pack.

Your wounded heart calls for a new fantastic
and my hands and my heart and my words answer.

Every day
you love me
I win the competition
that never happened.

Four Words

I waited
for your return.

I brooded
not important to you.

Friends of four months
you met twice
now a third time
are more important
than 20 years.

More important
than 30 years.

Another 30 minutes
before packing.

A note
when you return,
if you return,
only a note.

But not 30 minutes more.

Instead
Your four words:

"I missed you … physically"

And everything
absolutely everything
changed

forever.

What I Want from You

You know I love you.
Obviously.

And you may know I admire you and your strength
Maybe more than I admire anyone else.

You have gone through stuff
No one should have to go through.
Too much of that stuff, too many ways, too many times.
And you have chosen to be happy.

Many others have gone through similar stuff
And it has broken or embittered them or worse.

You are a rock and I admire your strength.
A rock

But, as strong as you are,
You are still human.
And there have to be days, hours, or whatever
When you feel broken and damaged
And it is just too much.

We all do.

What I want from you

Is that sometime
when you feel that way –

That you cannot take any more of it
Are exhausted
Drained
Broken
Hollow and empty
And all you want is to cry and sob and let the despair sweep over you

That you will cry and sob and despair
On my shoulder
In my arms
And let me be with you when you feel no hope
For a while.
And know it is okay
To be with me and know I know you are still a rock.

That is all I want from you.

Pissed Off to Perfect

In my pain
and suffering
and most of all, my self-absorption,
I mentioned
our 30 years together.

I'm sure
the context was
how I have earned better treatment from
you
than I was receiving
at the moment.
And maybe, at the moment
in the moment,
all of the time.

My familiar theme
with those intimate with me:
my monkey mind
frames a world for me
that doesn't work
for anyone.

Not too gently,
at least in my perception,
you pointed out that
It was only 20 years.
Ouch.

But soon,
through the magic of who you are
and maybe the magic
of who I am
when I'm with you,
30 years became
still one more
fun joke between us.

Through the magic
of who you are
and maybe a bit of
the magic
of who I am when I'm with you.

Rainy Day in the Office

Sunday.
Rainy day in the office,
with myself,
writing, thinking, dreaming.

No one, well almost no one,
knows where I am
and can reach me
with emergencies,
tempting invitations,
completely appropriate requests.

Rainy day in the office,
finishing the leftover bottle
of Billecart-Salmon Brut Rosé,
the one and a half, oops I thought there were more,
leftover chocolates from Sciascia Confections,
and thinking of you.

It doesn't get any better than that.
Well, there is one-way
it could get better than that.

If Only

If only

Two words
Stealth joy-killer,
Self-talk mantra
Whining, complaining
Self-absorption

All that's needed
For a perfect relationship
With you
For my happiness

Almost nothing for you to do

Trivial for you to do
To complete our relationship
For my joy
For your joy
When you do it

Too selfish to speak … unfair to ask

Too risky to ask
And if you say ”no”
Destroyer of relationship

And only the first drop
In an ocean of
If onlys

With you
There are
No *if onlys*

Moody Son-of-a-Bitch 1

From her
Words never sting

Is it she?
Or is it I? – naa, not,“me” – “I”

Rhyming may be nice
Maybe necessary

And bad grammar rhymes so
Much better
Than saying it right …correctly.

Is she special in some way?
The list groans under the burdensome
Ring of banal squawking – words sounding so common

So empty
Of the realty I live with her

Or am I just
Special when I am with her?

So *That's* What Everyone is Talking About

So far, my muse has not
walked across the bar
with a beer in each hand

And said to me
"Tell me what you love.
Tell me all about it."

Maybe someday
That will happen to me.

Until it does
I will console myself with
The day you said

So THAT'S what everybody's been talking about!

Actually, I don't need
Any consolation.
I can buy my own beer
And sit with my memories

With appreciation for "Muse" by Bill Van Buskirk

RELATIONSHIPS

(BEING IN AND OUT OF RELATIONSHIPS)

Afterglow

After I healed, after we healed
I discovered, we discovered
We could heal after the damage
Of clumsy words spoken from fear.

Fear of not being good enough
Of competing with a ghost and
  with the wrong person at the right time
Of loving unselfishly

Of not hearing from love
From the security of being loved
From the patience of being loved
From the wisdom of being loved.

And so afterglow
Became part of our culture
A word that crystallizes our joy
Reminds us of our love
Signals our growth together.

Earned through pain
Patience
Fear.

Like so much
Of our relationship

Moody Son-of-a-Bitch 4

There IS a
Moody son-of-a bitch
Story

Maybe it will find its way
To us
Some day.
Maybe now.

Music cruise,
Train waiting for your morning walk
Almost not our morning walk
Could it have been never?

Vulnerable
Running away
From myself
Almost again

Your anger
How DARE I spoil your joy
How Dare I.

You waited so long for this
You earned it
So many hard times

How Dare I?

The tone of Greta
Child, adult, saint, avenger, prophet, Cassandra
Shouting into Davos' dead ears

How Dare I?
Not hear your words
Your pain
Your truth
Shouting into my awakening ears

And hearing my love for you
In another way
Over and over and over again.

Playboy Magazine 1

Playboy Magazine
had wonderful, one-page stories.
Maybe it still does.
I have not looked recently

50 years ago, a story:
A traveler's late-night misfortune
An elegant, secluded mansion

The butler, smelling slightly of sulfur,
welcomes him, seemingly unsurprised,
and leads him through the exquisitely furnished rooms
up the staircase to the beautiful mistress of the home.

Of course, they make love –
Wonderful love -
Hey, it IS a Playboy story –
And then she tells her story.

She hated being ugly,
at least in her own eyes,
and sold her soul to the devil
or maybe it was a devil's assistant
for three wishes.

To be the most beautiful woman in the world:
And the devil made her the most beautiful 100-year-old woman in the world.

To have wealth beyond imagining:
And since there is no wealth beyond imagining,
the devil gave her nothing.

Down to wish number three

Then the master stroke:
To be loved unselfishly.

For decades I pitied that poor devil, smelling slightly of sulfur, or maybe his assistant:
Welcoming this stranger, and then another and another,
To make love with the woman he loved
While he waited, lonely and jealous.

And then I found myself, many years ago,
Falling in love with a woman I could never be with,
and chose ever so intentionally, to love her unselfishly, forever.

And it worked

For me, for her, for all around us.

Making life so simple
so complex,
so good.

Playboy Magazine 2

Slow learner that
I feel I am – often –
I decided
the devil
or maybe it was his assistant,
did not suffer

when the woman he loved --
unselfishly --
made love to stranger after stranger
that he brought to her.

And still later – much, much later -- I thought
maybe the devil made love with her also.

And still later,
maybe she felt he was the best lover in her world,
forever.

Maybe.

I Don’t Know How to Tell You

I don’t know how to tell you
I’m in love
With someone else

No words come to me

I don’t know how to tell you
How it happened

It’s not your fault
I didn’t plan it
I didn’t intend it
I didn’t want it

Because I had no idea
What it was

I don’t know how to tell you
I’m in love

I still love you
But I’m not in love with you

At least
Not in love with you
In the way
I love her

I didn't plan it
Because
I didn't know what it was
Until it happened

I don't know how to tell you
I'm in love
with someone else

No words exist

There are no words
to say
I'm in love
With someone else

I don't know how anyone can tell
a lover
I am in love with someone else

Nothing

Sometimes
    in life
    in relationship
    in love

We do things
    so the other will do things

In a relationship,
    or maybe only a single event
    among other single events,
I do this
    so you will do that.

We engage in transactions.

With you,
    for me, there are no transactions.

What I do with you, for you,
    I do for the joy of doing it
    you do not owe me anything
    You never owe me anything

All of my actions with
    you are complete in themselves

They may lead to some things

and we may be
able to predict
those somethings

But what I am doing
is not for
those somethings
they often lead to

We can say they are complete
in and of themselves.
but they are not for
whatever happens next

Maybe that's what loving is all about.

I never do anything with you
so you will do something with me

Not doing it for you
so you will do whatever for me.

Well, maybe
There are
Occasional exceptions.

That Never Was

A relationship that never was
Like so many other
relationships that never were

A surprise kiss
A greeting
On a Saturday morning
A day, early in our relationship,
Set aside for play together

But the surprise greeting
A kiss– – On the lips– –
First ever, quick and nice
But different and with a message I missed

In the pleasure of being together
Innocent fun
Followed by years just like it
But without that kiss
Ever again

The kiss was an invitation
Offered spontaneously and innocently
But coming from where you were
And in a way I didn't recognize

A kiss, just one kiss, almost the only one
Ever

That held the message
I didn't recognize at the time

So later
It was too late
To get
What I later wanted

So things evolved
As they needed to

You went through
What you went through
It gave you
For a while
What you wanted
And then it was over
Forever

And finally
"Finally" only in the sense of
Forever,
We both got
Much more than
We could have hoped
If I had recognized
What that kiss
was really saying.

Crater to Culture

In relationships,
bumps in the road happen.
Some become craters
damaging or ending
the relationship.
Some become pebbles
barely noticed and so very hard to recall.

Somehow, we discovered how to handle
the bumps that turned into craters
almost ending our relationship forever
as had happened to me with others
over and over again.

Somehow, we did the hard work
of turning craters into culture,
prized, beloved, experiences of
learning and growth --
part of our humor together --
visited often in a fountain of jokes

as we grew closer and closer
building a shared culture,
one-liners of
laughter and love,
toward becoming one.

Feb 12, 2021

The Measure

The measure of who I am

Is who you are

When you are with me.

The measure of who you are

Is who I can be

When I am with you.

100 Ways

In every moment of
intimacy
there are 100 ways we can speak of
what we feel

what is happening
what did happen
what might happen
what we want
what we don't want.

We are always at choice in what we say
and the world that it creates
for ourselves and for others.

We are always at choice in what we say.
We forget that
and we are afraid to admit that
and we are ashamed to admit that.
To ourselves.
To others.

We are always at choice
in what we say
and the world that it creates
for ourselves and for others.

And we free ourselves and others
when we admit that.

Fuckbuddies

We missed our chance.
We could have been fuckbuddies
when you needed the solace and rapture
of fantastic sex.

Perhaps over and over again
When you were most passionate
And your body could yearn for
And deliver as much sex as you might wish.

We could have been fuckbuddies
When my body could have come through for you
When I was in my young prime
-- Probably not as primey as I now think --

When life for me was all about
Love-making over and over
Whenever.

I dream that we could have been
Fuckbuddies
And you would remember how great
We were as fuckbuddies
Together.

And you found a fuckbuddy

And it was fantastic
For a while
Until it wasn't

When you both tried
For more
And those days went away
Forever.

And I was not ready
Too many obligations
Two obligations
To others
But not to me

So, we were never fuckbuddies
and never will be.

Yet I keep wishing for them
though I know that
what we found is better.

So very, very much better
Forever.

The Drip, Drip, Drip

The

drip

drip

drip

of vodka

and its friends

off your liver

has turned

my heart

to stone.

Deatheater

In my life,
maybe in yours,
comes the deatheater
too often
wrapping me in words
eating away my soul,
all of it.

Words that leave
me hollow,
empty,
sorrowful,
hating myself for listening
over
and over
and over again.

SELF …AS IN SELF-ABSORBED

Waiting for Raul

I thought opening groups
played for only
20, maybe 30 minutes.

This group
continues forever
it seems.

Are there really
two equally billed
main acts?
On this chilly night?

Twice as much is half as much
or less.

Will the Mavericks ever show up?
And when they finally do,
will they ever end
on this chilly night?

Two Worlds

Why are there two worlds?
One filled with folks
who think I am
shallow,
over-rated,
unskilled,
incompetent
just another smoke-and-mirrors?

And another world
seemingly filled with folks
who over-rate me,
think
and expect
me to do
things I know I cannot do,
give me credit for what
they think I have done
and they like?

And why do I believe those first folks
and not the other

LOVE AND OTHER SCARY THINGS

Fear

I'm afraid
to tell you
what I want.

You might do
what I want
only because
I want it.

But I don't really want it.
I want only
to know
you want it.

I Can't Tell You

I can't tell you
how much
I love you.

I can't tell you
how much
I need you.

You might
run screaming
searching
for relief,
for daylight.

You could not respect
anyone so weak.
So, I can't tell you
how much
I love you

how much
I need you.

Want You to Know

I want you to know,
I want to tell you,
I want you to hear
how strong I am.

That I'll be okay
no matter what.

That you can tell me anything
though it may hurt,
for no reason you can guess.
But I'll be okay.

Some things you say
have nothing
to do with me,
and yet I use them
to hurt myself
for no reason.

I'm afraid to tell you
that I can hurt myself
with your words
because I'm afraid
you may choose your words too carefully
And I'll lose your sharing.

And so I want you to know
how strong I am
and you can say anything
and everything.
And I'll be okay.

That's what I want
and the chance to tell you
how weak
and vulnerable
and scared
I am.

That I just want my mother
to hold me and tell me
everything will be okay.

And for you to be my mom
and hold me
and tell me
everything will be okay.

And you do that every day
you are with me.
So now I can tell you
what you may not know
as you hold me.

SUSTAINABILITY (PAINED WORDS WRITTEN ABOUT UNSUSTAINABILITY)

Comments on the 411-Pound Gorilla

The ever-growing gorilla reminds me of the ever-increasing levels of CO2 in our atmosphere.

This poem was first written in 2010 and was titled "The 409-pound gorilla." It was retitled a few times. This month it might be titled: "The 417-pound gorilla."

The generally recognized calculations have been that when atmospheric CO2 levels exceeded 350 ppm global warming and climate change impacts would start occurring and would worsen if the levels of atmospheric CO2 concentration continued to rise.

In 1986 the 350 ppm level was reached and broached.

https://www.downtoearth.org.in/news/environment/world-breached-safe-atmospheric-co2-levels-33-years-ago-64546

417.04 Atmospheric CO2 for July 30, 2022. https://www.co2.earth/daily-co2

Data for retitling the poem are available at:

https://gml.noaa.gov/webdata/ccgg/trends/co2/co2_mm_mlo.txt

407.90 ppm May 2016

385.22 ppm May 2006

365.25 ppm May 1996

350.52 ppm May 1986

The 411-Pound Gorilla

The 411-pound gorilla
sits in the back of our classrooms
eating
and belching
and farting.

Ignored
by ourselves
our students
our colleagues
our deans
and our presidents.

As we keep our heads
buried in the sand
seeking success
in
business as usual.

Ignoring
the muffled pleas
of our grandchildren
and children
and our hearts.

jafstoner

Rachel Carson

My friend's thesis draft
speaks to me
in Rachel Carson's words to her friend
as she finished *Silent Spring*

"I think I let you see last summer
what my deeper feelings are about this
when I said I could never again listen
happily to a thrush song
if I had not done all I could.
And last night the thought of all the birds
and other creatures
and all the loveliness that is in nature
came to me with such a surge of deep
happiness,
that now I had done what I could -
I had been able to complete it –
now It had its own life. "

Speaks to me
saying maybe
somehow
I can be more than
Just
Smoke and mirrors.
Maybe

Charles Koch

There is no danger
Ayn Rand-inspired
Charles Koch
will be immortalized by historians
as the greatest murderer of all time
for extinguishing our own and all other species

on a planet turned into a red-hot cinder
from the “great hoax” of climate change
and global warming.

The hoax that released the methane from the tundra,
then from the seabed.

Government was the evil,
the *Road to Serfdom*,
so it must be destroyed.

But if there is climate change,
global warming,
we might need government
to survive.

So there must not be
climate change
and global warming.

And there is no serfdom
on a dead planet.

There is no danger
that Ayn Rand-inspired
Charles Koch
will be immortalized by historians
as the greatest murderer of all time
because there will be no historians
to chronicle our demise and his
contribution.

BLACK LIVES MATTER (PAINED WORDS ABOUT RACISM)

•

Two Drew Brees poems
An Explanation:

The two Drew Brees poems were written in immediate response to an incident involving Drew Brees, an American Football Hall of Fame quality quarterback.

In an interview, Mr. Brees made a careless statement in an otherwise caring interview in which he which he spoke passionately about his love for America. He was widely, and explosively, quoted as saying: "I will NEVER disrespect the flag by kneeling." https://www.youtube.com/watch?v=f3qQV2CtmuQ

Almost immediately he discovered that he had misunderstood what Colin Kapernick's kneeling during the American National Anthem really stood -- uprightly and courageously – for. In the minds of many Americans, Mr. Kapernick's kneeling does not disrespect America and the flag but is a pained protest at seemingly endless police brutality against people of color and systemic racism throughout America's history and present

At the time of the incident the pandemic was so severe that there was a possibility that the 2020 National Football League season might be cancelled. Thus the words

When football is back

maybe

The next day, Mr. Brees apologized for not understanding what the kneeling meant and means to many Americans of any color.

The news frenzy around the incident also brought to light what a really decent human being Mr. Brees is and how much he has contributed to the community in which he lives and played football so well.

The second poem was written when Mr. Brees made it clear that he had a new understanding of what Mr. Kapernick's and others' kneeling is really all about.

Drew Brees and Our Choices

Come September
When football is back
Maybe
And flags wave and anthems are sung
For sure.

We can choose
how we interpret
our actions and with whom
we stand or kneel.

When football is back
Maybe
And flags wave and anthems are sung
For sure.

Our choice is an interpretation,
only an interpretation,
nothing written in scripture,
nothing in the Constitution
says what standing or kneeling MEANS,
only whatever interpretation
we and others choose.

When football is back
Maybe
And flags wave and anthems are sung
For sure.

We can choose to stand with those
who chose to interpret
cynically, or blindly, or naively, or deafly
Colin Kaepernik's kneeling to protest racism
And societally permitted police brutality
as dishonoring a flag and an anthem
that happen to wave and sound.
Or we can kneel to honor those
whose lives and careers and homes and children
have been threatened and taken
by the racism and brutality Kaepernik and we
are protesting
as we kneel.

When football is back
Maybe
And flags wave and anthems are sung
For sure.

Words Strung Along the Left Margin
June 4, 2020

Drew Brees – 2

Drew Brees
Benefactor of New Orleans,
Super Bowl champion,
Hall of Fame quarterback,
Father, husband, son, friend to many,
Was a good, decent, caring person
When he spoke carelessly
On June 3, 2020.

Drew Brees
Benefactor of New Orleans,
Super Bowl champion,
Hall of Fame quarterback,
Father, husband, son, friend to many,
Was a good, decent, caring
Even better person
When he spoke humbly and courageously
On June 4, 2020.

Thank you, Mr. Brees
For showing all of us
We never stand taller
And earn respect faster
Than when we admit our error
And make amends.

Targets on Their Backs

Why don't we get it?

When a police officer
in Minneapolis
or St. Louis
or Louisville
or anywhere
else

Brutalizes or murders
anyone
and gets away with it

He or she
puts a target
on the back
of every police officer

In McAllen
the Bronx
Fayetteville
and everywhere
else

Why don't we get it?

July 4, 2020

POLITICS (WORDS WRITTEN ABOUT THE PRESENT AND PAST)

When?

When

will Republican Senators

find a woman

who passes a lie detector test

more credible

than a man

who refuses

to take one?

Written in *honor* of Professor Anita Hill and Ms. Blasey Ford.

Never, Never, Never Forget

When you feel a bit down
about some things
America did
or did not do,

Please never, never, never, forget
how lucky the world was
that America first discovered
the nuclear bomb

And
was the only nation
with a nuclear monopoly.

That it was not
Hitler and the Nazis,
or Stalin and his henchmen,
or Hideki Tojo and the militarists
who became the world's
nuclear monopolist in 1945.

Never, never, never forget
how lucky all of us still are.

WORDS ABOUT WORDS

Ode to Ted Hughes

When two wives
In a row
Stick their heads
In the oven,
There's probably
Something
Something wrong
With the husben

Poem's Measure

It is not the rhyming

Not the meter

Not the voice

That measure the poem.

It is those who

Discover the courage to write

Their first poem

In response.

Poetry and Sex

In sharing poems by
Bill Van Buskirk
with a friend,
the answer to a question
I never thought to ask came up.

How is poetry like sex?

There is another poem,
maybe many poems,
within that question,
squirming, pulsing, scratching,
yearning to get out,
to survive.

So many ways
that poetry
is like sex.
So many ways
poetry is not like sex.

However, for me
the answer that came up
before the question arose
that I had never asked
is so simple.

Poetry is more fun with the right partner.

Words Strung along the Left Margin

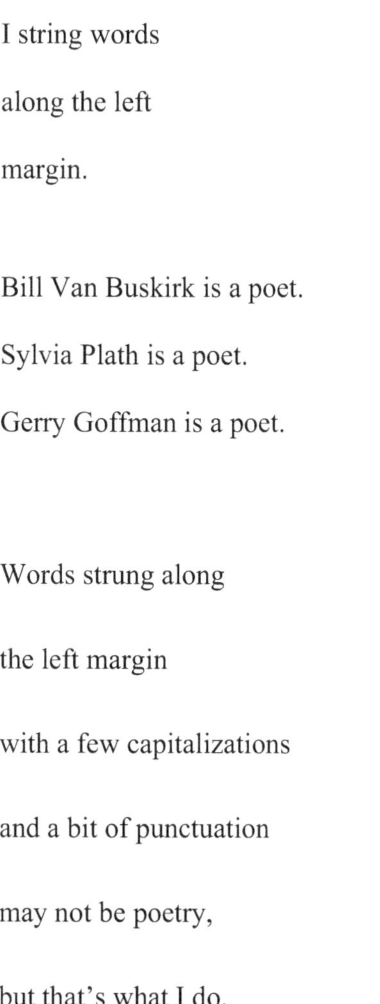

I string words

along the left

margin.

Bill Van Buskirk is a poet.

Sylvia Plath is a poet.

Gerry Goffman is a poet.

Words strung along

the left margin

with a few capitalizations

and a bit of punctuation

may not be poetry,

but that's what I do.

The Lover Behind the Words

The grand old poet says, "So you write
poetry too?"
And I teeter in the doorway of love and
fear.

A put-down, exposing my pretensions and
arrogance
as I stand next to greatness,
hoping some of the light will reflect and
illuminate me.
My inadequacy so poorly hidden,
just retribution for my chutzpah.

Or was it love?
A remembrance of her early, lonely,
unsure days.
a welcoming embrace and caring hug.
"Yes, we have all been there.
Don't judge yourself.
Don't listen for praise from others.
Just do it.
A poet is someone who writes.
That's all there is to it."

How many times I have heard the putdown
and not the loving invitation?
Made a challenger, an antagonist,
of the lover behind the words?

With appreciation to Bill van Buskirk for "Beasts" and for "Shopping for Diamonds on South Street."

Poetry

For me
Poetry is rich and subtle
Flowery in phrasing
Full of mystery and hidden meaning

Lyrical and lilting
Beyond my capabilities
Even to imagine

So, I may never write poetry
And I may never be a poet
And I'm fine with that

And maybe poetry speaks from the vulnerable heart
Seeking another listening heart
In forgiveness and compassion
I can write that

Even if it's not poetry

WISDOM

Heaven

I have always wanted to be a Renaissance person

and know everything.

The last person

to hold all known

knowledge in his mind.

I thought heaven was where

you could ask any what-if question –

What if I actually got that divorce

and joined the woman I was coming to love?

What if I had walked up Riverside Drive

and not down Tiemann Place that day?

What if the Nazis had invaded Britain successfully

and won the war?

And know the answer.

Late in life

I decided I was almost

correct.

But a wee bit off.

Knowing all those what-if answers

would be hell.

What Remains

Physical objects
Get Broken
Lost
Stolen
And something else – it slipped my mind

Memories
Get forgotten
Distorted
Obscured
And something else I also forgot

Relationships
Pass away
Are grown out of by ourselves or others
Are moved-on from
End in pain
And sometimes endure
Sometimes,

But what always remains?

A subtle, hidden but deep feeling
Of warm, caring connectedness
A sense that we are "good enough"
Even though
We cannot describe it,
Cannot identify were it came from,

Recall the event or person that triggered it,
Figure out why it cannot be turned into a concrete impression
With a time and date attached to it

But it is always there,
Consoling, strengthening, healing us.
Always remaining there for us
When we most need it
And when we don't.
Always remaining.

Kurt Vonnegut and Joseph Heller

I read someplace that

Kurt Vonnegut once asked

Joseph Heller, at the lavish

estate of some mogul or other,

"What does it feel like to be

with someone who made more money

in one day than you made

from all of your successful books

in your lifetime?"

And Heller replied:

"I have something he will never have."

Vonnegut: "Oh?"

"The knowledge that I have enough."

FINIS

Spring Lived in Her Smile

Spring lived in her smile

She was the summer and fall

Without her: winter

June 5, 1969 --- July16, 2022

Jim was awakened to poetry when he heard his friend Bill Van Buskirk recite "Shopping for diamonds on South Street", during an Organizational Behavior Teaching Conference in 1998. Soon after, he started reading the poetry of Sylvia Plath, Ted Hughes, and others. His first poem occurred shortly after he walked past a couple sitting in a sports car waiting for a traffic light to change and listening to, most likely, a Beatles song. That 1995 event occurred as he was walking to his hotel after a set of meetings at the Academy of Management Annual Meeting in Montréal. He really liked that poem, and he lost it.

Words strung along the left margin is Jim's first book of poems.

www.ingramcontent.com/pod-product-compliance
Lightning Source LLC
LaVergne TN
LVHW010108170826
845678LV00012B/2299

9798844211966